Locating Strongwoman

Tolu Agbelusi

This edition first published in Great Britain 2020
Jacaranda Books Art Music Ltd
27 Old Gloucester Street,
London WC1N 3AX
www.jacarandabooksartmusic.co.uk

A CIP catalogue record for this book is available from the British
Library

ISBN: 9781913090135
eISBN: 9781913090333

Cover Image: Copyright © Carrie Mae Weems.
Courtesy of the artist and Jack Shainman Gallery, New York
Cover Design: Rodney Dive
Typeset by: Kamillah Brandes

Printed and bound by CPI Group (UK) Ltd, Croydon, CR0 4YY

this is the tale
I keep on telling
trying to get it right:
the feast of women,
the feeding and
being fed.

—lucille clifton

Contents

I

II

III

I

"Don't you see? I am shedding my skins."

—VIEVEE FRANCIS,
'Another Antipastoral'

Faking Death To Avoid Sex Is Not Extreme

Death is a mating ritual
—the base of my wings hacked,
a male seizing my body
mid-flight. It's a vice,
spiny claspers from a dragonhunter
who doesn't care that his iron hold
gouges my eyes, pierces my head,
splits my chitin.

This is a death I can come back from
only if I'm quick—freeze
midair, plunge to ground or vegetation,
make a corpse of my body,
let the hunter hover
for as long as it will take him
to believe I have perished
or at least that I cannot be coerced
into being prey.

Does it matter if I am always escaping?
If I can't let myself be carefree?
Sister damselfly changed the rules,
colluded with evolution to turn
her green stripes blue to mimic
males, trick them away
from harassment. It worked
for a while.

I may lose a limb in the fall
but if he ceases pursuit, do I not win?
Is this not how we practise being strong?
Breaking ourselves in pieces
so we can choose the one
fragment that stays whole?

Timeline

After Franny Choi

I

I stumbled into the first like a warm shower—each strand of water gliding across my body paused at the smallest grooves, an exercise in savouring delicacy. I never thought I could be pleasure. I wanted to possess that feeling. So I let him fall on me. Through me. In me. But I was just practice. Soon, his *Baby you know thinking is not your strong point* would scald where he once soothed, dissolve my voice to nothing more than the steam puffing my cheeks—luggage in a room I never opened. I didn't leave. He visited me in Paris, introduced me to his *friend*, and didn't hide his pining, didn't shame when later he touched my body and didn't see me. Watching her through my face, he entered my body—dry and writhing.

II

I stumbled into the second like my favourite dish in a stranger's kitchen after a seven-day juice fast. Seven mouthfuls in, I wondered when he too would turn to poison—who I'd have to become to keep him spelled. We would disappear into the TV, poems he would read, steamed car windows behind tall grass bushes, meals he would cook. Questions he would ask, as if trying to tell me without saying out loud that he wanted no one else. He must have seen the scars, how they snagged my feet and held me from running into his arms. He must have wondered how long it would take before I didn't see glimpses of the first boy and all the nameless ones between, inside his mistakes. Does this matter? Does the wife who walked in on us one morning matter?

Recipe Book

Mother's old lined notebook,
dough-stained and well worn,
was the first ingredient.
Its sighting fired the leaping rhythm
in my feet. Had me jump into an apron,
on a stool to lift me closer to the worktop,
to my mother who would read instructions
I wanted to follow. Often I powdered us both
with carelessly poured flour. She would draw
shapes on my cheeks in the haze, before watching
me mix eggs, sugar, whatever came next.
I was still allowed rough edges, still allowed
to lick the batter from the bowl without regard
for appearances. There was patience then.

Frankly I Am Running Out of Ways to Fight For You

If it wasn't him, it was someone like him—
promising luxury, spending your money for sport.
He was no match for you. I affirmed your worth. Tried.
You preferred to dote on his blunders. As if you knew the love
he promised was so unsteady, any critique was a threat
to your dream of belonging. Is that why you couldn't leave?

He held your heart with barbed wire. Made you believe
his barbs were a necessary test to prove you were worthy of him.
He shuttled women to your bed, brandished their youth like a threat
he knew would ignite your insecurities. Everyone but you could spot
his lies easy—only tarred section of a potholed highway. *Love*
he said, squeezing your face between his hands and you tried

to forget *stupid*, *weak*, the names he gave you. Aren't you tired?
I held your trembling body in a park where once-green leaves
compliantly fell from their branches—a cycle of survival. *Love*
yourself enough to walk away I said, *to survive him.*
But performing contentment to spite the other women was sport,
winnable—your whole self summoned as a formidable threat.

If only you had the same audacity, not to shrink for him. Threaten
his foothold. There were ways. I unpacked them. Tried.
A stack of compliments was all it took to deter you—one skewed spot
to obscure your view. I refined your angle of sight, wanted to believe
it was enough to dismantle the persona you clung to, which wasn't him.
But you concocted lies to feign blindness to the reasons you shouldn't love

him. As if he wasn't a bed of nails your love
laid on. Keening. When his hurt stabbed your bones, I treated
each wound until we broke your resolve to endure him,
crave external permission to acknowledge your own voice. I tried
to revive your season of *this is who I am take it or leave*
it. And didn't we reminisce on days when you'd sport

red hair, blue lips and a bald head, daring men to spot
the difference between their fantasies and the real you, when I tried
to make you blend, it was you who said they had to learn to love
only the you they met or leave. Those days, when you believed
you deserved more. When the thought of lonely was not a threat
that made you surrender sense to the nearest ogling man, him.

When you demanded your card and keys at the spot where you met him,
I need to learn to love me you said, a dormant threat till then. I believed
for you. Why abrade the scar before it heals, cleave yet again to him. I tried.

We All Take Risks Stepping Into Thin Air

My first night in Cayenne, I slept with a man I met
at the airport (another teacher). His bed a hair's breadth
from my misgivings, his only preoccupations were sleep

and cheap accommodation. When he moved
on, the bartender floated a drink to my room. Cracked
a joke. Poured his tongue into my mouth, promised

to return at 1am, said I would discover him.
Because I believed him, I barricaded the door, snuffed
out the lights and lay still until he tired of knocking.

Razor in the Oesophagus

Each time a muscle clenches, I sink
into the soft, pink, tissue of your throat,
perforate and frill its smooth silk,
enjoying how blood twirls a dress
onto my flat and straight body,
as though celebrating.
It was you who steered me
past the ridges of your palate.
A doctor trips over razor blade. Calls me
'foreign object' instead. Says
your body is fighting. Still fighting.

Isn't this what you wanted
—your name on every tongue?

She Wears Beauty as Costume. Happiness Too.

Her eyes provoke
for an answer. She sucks sinkholes
under her cheek bones, rotates
her head in a circular motion
still interrogating her reflection,
expecting it to read her mind. She unfolds
a tool belt of brushes and foams, shimmering
face paint, too light and too dark until blotted
—beige semicircle under her eyes
controlling brown everywhere
else and then golds, reds and layers of paint and thick
layers of paint. The mirror would like to talk about
a lesson on evolution. But she's smiling,
putting words into its mouth.

My Mother Says Our Relationship Feels Official

1

Her mind tells her she's loved me deeply.
My eyes remain steady until she takes my hands,
claps them together between her palms and asks
for keys to a love that doesn't feel like duty.
She's asking to learn. I want to forget the pain
enough to say something that absolves us both.
I don't know what to say.

2

I felt naked each time when, scanning
head to toe, she would explain me to her guests,
encourage me to be another girl. The daughter
she wanted.

Smile more. Speak louder. Be less

blunt. More open. Less naïve. Mingle,
like the others. How do you expect
to make friends, attract men, be liked, be...

All those times she looked at me
and only saw what wasn't.
Her eyes now dare to hold me hostage.

3

I am sorry
my love is not all limbs and giggles
that my smile is a slow bloom.

I am sorry that I don't linger
in crowded rooms. That my voice
doesn't lend itself to high pitches,
easy jokes and a pheremoning lightness.

You will find me in the silences between
conversations, short phrases dropping timely
and heavy, a hail of awkwardness that cracks
into unexpected laughter. There are people
who pull life from this. For whom I'm enough.

4

I love my mother.
My mother loves me.
We rarely speak
the same language.

Soldier Ants

I was eight when ants invaded
my bed, burrowed a hole
through my window net, marched
until my white sheets blackened
with their oversized heads. Thousands
of them matted in a black cloud,
clamping into my skin—
a gradual, constant burning.

I'm 36 now. Haven't forgotten.
Whenever life creeps up and tramples,
they loom—the lover who forgot
to remove his wedding band, the boss
who said bye with a letter on my desk,
the job centre queue every Tuesday—

the ants   they multiply.

Nothing Happened

"I drew a line. When I went further, I drew a new line
and then another line."
—*Toon Tellegen tr. Judith Wilkinson*

My car was broken. His offer was my safest
option on a starless night. I didn't ask
for the beach detour, I tripped
into his humour, into the mesh of his vast knowledge.
Nothing happened.

&

I wanted to talk. I knew he'd understand. Didn't
expect him to hold my hand in the brazen sun,
or quicken my breath without invitation. Not
in the middle of a bustling market. Only words
were exchanged. I staggered backwards
when his lips tried to mingle. I swear.
I even deleted his number.

&

I blame the moon. How it lit the navy blue
of his uniform, set stage for his bright
white teeth, primed the copper of his skin
just right. I blame God. The almighty
was admiring his handiwork, the beauty of him
his confidence, the authority in his stride, I had
no choice. I too watched him work.
Nothing happened.

&

We hiked to the end of our breaths
behind the tall grass to see
how far we could go before sundown.
It was just the once.

He calls. I lose my body in the pool
of his chest. I'm learning how to swim.
I am.

II

What Kind of girl are you?
The kind of girl who wants to live, I said, and I
did want to
until I didn't anymore.

—VIEVEE FRANCIS, 'Taking It

II

Fall

As it was, struggling to rise
with violence and failing,
his impotence
was her ransom.

If the fall didn't drown
him with shame,
if shame didn't drive
him away, that night
would have been:
            —old man suckling
at granddaughter's breasts
            —screams trying, failing
to break free, skin rising
like pine needles.

How It Begins

When I play the number game, demand a report
of forty hands on the white rectangular tables,
Ayesha goes missing. I say *200 fingers*
and the noise of 190 fingers banging the tables
sends visible shivers through Ayesha. Blink

and I'd have missed her spring from her seat
before catching herself. Pushing her body
back into the chair, hands pressed into her lap.

Usually, even before my ruler attempts to summon
silence by slapping the white from a blackboard
she would be pencil sharp, book open, expectant
against the chaos in my class of twenty ten-year-olds.
Later, the class teacher offered me answers. Strolling home

yesterday, Ayesha didn't notice Jamie and his little brother
until he grabbed her hands and rammed
her back into the dust. Edged her panties aside for a dagger
of fingers. Her teeth clamped into the tiny hands covering
her mouth. Rumour says he screamed louder than her. He

is only seven. After lunch when I see Ayesha, she is staring
into space again, as if mourning what Jamie stole.
The moment he enters the classroom, her face
hardens. On another day, the glares thrust
between them would have passed for child's play.
But today...

When class is over Ayesha transfers her books
into a backpack. She is already practicing
a life of walking the tightrope
between a silence that chokes
and a silence
that (will make believe it) is a sanctuary.

Locating Strongwoman

After Carrie Mae Weems 'The Kitchen Table Series'

Hands placed just so, I instructed the mirror to document transformation—becoming my mother with nothing more than a gesture and the sheen of bright red gloss. Who knew ten years later, I'd avoid mirrors that dared throw her in my face. Did I say all mirrors? Except I was crashing them against concrete, finding the sharpest shard, digging into my skin for a rush of crimson, an untainted reflection... Hospital windows wouldn't break. I'd know. That was a long time ago. In this decade, my mother's hands are less steady. I stand behind her. Frame her hands in mine and pull the lipstick across. The mirror looks at us. I don't avoid her eyes staring from my face and hers at the same time. How could I? I've lived long enough to know what it took to be her.

Belle

A daughter hell-bent on gorging herself
with computer generated beauty. A daughter
who refuses to see herself. Who can't,

not when she pledges devotion
to no carbs, no fat, low proteins, no balance, stomach
pounding from want, skin dissolving from bones—

when at last she agrees to listen, not to her mother
but to me, her mother's friend, if I shadow her footsteps
to the kitchen, wrap an arm around her poking clavicle,

I will reveal I hated my body once, wide thighs, broad nostrils,
all of it. If I keep the silence until her disbelief thaws,
she may ask a question. Then another. If I extend a mirror

and at last she sees herself in caricature, if the questions
continue, she is plotting the return of cushioned bones.
If, at that moment, her mother slumps in another room,

she is shedding the heaviness her body nurtured
those dark months of exhausting all her energy,
defying her daughter's plea to join the afterlife.

The Things I Can't Say I

I will hold on to your hand a touch longer
than is comfortable. *You are reaching too high
too soon, nobody will want you this way*—I have
not forgotten your admonition or the minute
of silence you held, on learning that someone
found me worthy of investment. I built
a whole city from words and put it on stage
like I told you I would. People came, found
parts of themselves staring back.

I once lifted a steaming pot with bare hands because
I saw my mother do it. Weeks after my fingertips
had grown new skin, I would learn that she escaped
burns by moving so quickly the pot was released
by the time her brain registered heat. I'm holding
on to your hands a shade longer than is comfortable.
What you get depends on how you give.

They Say You Gotta Let It Go

I scrub it out on the kitchen floor
hammer my knees into linoleum
let them bleed
the words my lips could have released.

I throw bleach on it.
Watch its striking edges dissolve or hide.
Hide.   In that space heavy from silence
where unresolved issues sit

                              waiting to be disturbed

by the next person who sees in my skin
good reason for a tone-dive
into condescension   a needling rudeness
I must ignore if ___,   ___,   ___.

I drown it out with music
screaming   at how often
I scrape its breath into my palm

and will it   to beat slower.   Forget
forget   forget   knowing each time
the assault birthing rage   the rage
is harder   to forget

Before the Bomb Blast... (Baga Massacres 2015)

Days before, dad tried to coax the girl out of me
with a gift. Nothing like the big girl pouch
from the uncles—stringy plasticine threads
like the ones in the film dad said I couldn't watch.
I peeped.

Red cable   Green cable
                          Noise
            Blood
                                          Bodies
Dust   I don't recall

if they offered it as gift or was it *come,*
wrap this pouch round your waist.
Obey, or mum's body sharpens the machete.
Dad's gift?
                        Pink frilly purse.

                  It was everything   but me
—preoccupied with straddling trees reserved
for long legged boys, twisting my stringy
ten-year-old body in poses that dropped my mother's jaw,

        obìrin bí ọkunrin, wedged halfway between
her admiration and disappointment   I said no

I   keep   going

back

to   one moment:

a phone startling my

body

        How often
I had folded into myself   a trigger
               awaiting
                        to my relevance
wanting
to grow   be centre

of something.   ~~Did I imagine~~ this was it ?   My torso
rocketing across the street.

Did I suspect the uncles

playing a game and walk like lead
was tucked in my trainers or was I just thinking
I must advance for mummy?
                 I can't remember
~~Rolling heads~~   the men
        ~~who'd suspected~~   my explosiveness.
~~I find~~ myself
                 running

~~back back back~~ back
to my father's lap.

This time when he gives me the purse,
all pink and bright, my face blossoms
as wide as a magnolia and holds its pose.

Maybe that way I wouldn't be

tussling with the meaning of   masu kunan bakin wake

kisan kai   ajónirun

Be a Lawyer They Said

You spend your days cradling death,
watching grief track its stages through faces.
First, it punctures the lacrimal.

The skin around the eyes will contort;
crepe paper sogging under
the force of drowning tears.

Soon it roars—a mournful pitch escaping
the body, uncontrolled, dragging,
wolf-like howls that don't relent.

A stream will overflow its banks.
Silently. It will crack the larynx,
still the face, leave it dead.

Except for the lips, pursed tightly,
holding back the sadness
threatening to break through.

All the while you grow
into a ministry—
laying on hands.

You did not train for this.

Ezekiel 37

Bones convalescing in a shallow grave
rattle alive when the alarm sings
I am not forgotten, I am not forgotten,
I am not forgotten, God knows my name.

I pull on a black tailored dress,
leather seamed to tell everyone
(including myself)
I didn't come to play.

Days like this demand strong lipstick.
Fenty's Griselda from the customised
gift box marked "armour for heavy days".

If I'm lucky, a sister will smile arms around
me on my commute, hold my gaze
long enough to make certain I feel seen.

Memory will lend me a strut, instruct
my feet—*move too fast to stop, to think,*
to collapse, to fall out. This is the dance.

When a shiver threatens
my delicate balance,
I will return

to the affirmation of waking moments,
random voice notes from praying sisters
who, sensing what I haven't uttered, urge:

wholeness will find its way back to your breath,
whatever is broken in you will heal, you will
remember who you are, until then, you will not
carry your bones alone.

Hallelujah (Hillsborough shorts 3)

Many times I've played this disaster.
Flirted with its intricacies in micro-frames
reversed it in milliseconds to catch his face.
I know this scene well.
His off-pink body rises against the wire mesh—
candy floss over sticks of hands raising him
like weak hallelujahs that fly and fall and crash
into body bags clad with eyes and the scent of life
leaving hurriedly. Today it supersedes work.
She is watching her father die in real time.
Slowed down. Zoomed in. Her legs become
a bobbing needle sewing twenty-six years of pain
into the carpet. The force jerking her shoulders
even as she struggles not to cry warns of a hurricane.
Beside her, I sit still.
Lock the doors to my uncle's 3-day-old corpse
that keeps exhuming itself from a personal world
that has no place in this boardroom. To disconnect
myself and bring her back to now, I touch her
just above the knees. I approach with caution, aware,
of the corralled storm still raging inside her. Inside me too.

Cento*

"Here, there is no place that doesn't see you."
—Rainer Maria Rilke tr. Stephen Mitchell

You are confronted with yourself
each year, eyes like ripening fruit.
The thirty-eighth year of my life.
I had not expected to be an ordinary
woman, plain as bread. Silence arrives like a servant
to tidy things up. I had expected
more. Such days when the sun's in a drawer
and the drawer is locked. I have forgotten
the why of everything. I sense an indifference
larger than anything. I had expected more than
this. I offer no apology. I will skip without your rope.
Since you say I should not, I will create my own.

What Exactly Do You Want To Know?

Though flaunting dazzling, royal blue necks,
Cassowaries prefer to keep a low profile.

If provoked they are capable
of inflicting injury. Sometimes fatal.

The factory of my body works
overtime. Ears, hands, shoulders, arms

skipping into wilful service for the few
who have taken the time to know me well.

When a Giant Himalayan Lily pushes its stalk
13 feet high, sprouts stunning trumpets of flowers

only the gardener will remember
the seven years it took to bloom.

The last time I found myself
in the middle of an ocean I swam

until I remembered
I couldn't swim. It has always been close

to impossible—pinning myself into a box,
asking others not to do the same.

III

"I did then what I knew how to do. Now that I know better, I do better."

—MAYA ANGELOU

Things I Can't Say II

How do you ask
to be crushed,
to hold the weight
of another on your chest
till you can only breathe
long and deep?
How do you explain
that your body must
be forced to expel all
its air, to let go,
that you are too accustomed
to leaning on solid things
that break without warning,
that you loved a man once
and only knew this as truth
the day your body leaned
so fully into his chest, you
could have been weightless,
that you chase that feeling,
the depth of that serenity,
sometimes in a hot bath
where the heat holds on
until you surrender,
sometimes under the weight
of a fat man who doesn't
love you, but has enough heft
to force your body to let go.

What the Girl Wants

Neon pink nubuck leather high-tops
beckoned from the shop window,
dripped their colour into my wanting,
enticed me inside the store. I slipped
my feet into the plush leather. My toes
breathed. I stood to walk and glided
instead, reminiscing on younger days
when shorts or the fanciest Sunday
dress were matched with white high-top
sneakers, *can't you see what the other girls
are wearing* said Mum, *don't you want to be pretty?*
I wanted to be comfortable, to loop
white laces into an underhand knot, run
without fear of stumbling. Left my heels
on the shop floor. Never went back.

Strongwoman

When Patrick told me I wanted him
promised he would be gentle, I said
no. (I did). *No*—my mouth didn't shoot
arrows. No knives. But I said *No*
I don't want to. No not tonight.
Patrick no.
Yes.   I like you but   stop
No.

                              Then silence

masked itself as permission

(It's what he'll say).

෫

When a random stranger
stroked my car door
all familiar, sliding himself
into my back seat
without invitation or introduction,
I hurled my voice:
get out! Get Out! GET OUT!   I hit
on third try.

When Dennis stole my research
for a boardroom showdown, I didn't
doubt the strength of my words
to humble him, I wove my voice
into a low even tone, lashed him calmly
question after question and didn't relent
when his answers lost their way, not until
he conceded the game I never agreed to play.

෫

But when Angelo's lips drove into mine,
I wondered if he would notice
there was no give, charge through anyway,
or stop? His hands scraped my thighs like
sandpaper, I must have made concrete of my body.
Angelo stopped.

Ça *va? Pleus pas euh. N'est pas obligé le sexe*
mais tu peut me faire une pipe quand meme.

I   froze. Choked
on guilt, on why I couldn't scream,
what I did to end up here again, questions
about this strength that fails
every time it really matters.

Strongwoman would have used both hands.
He would have begged.

I Found Home

I met a man who could have been
any man, only he wasn't. What kind
of absurdity makes one want to spend
time learning an obscure language?
He became fluent. In me. For the sake
of it. Invested enough time to decipher
my laughter dialects—pure release,
stuttered in warning, muddied with
questions, or cluttered with doubt. He
studied every detail convinced
he was reviving a city we could call home.
Came alive accumulating vocabulary,
connecting them like puzzle patterns.
When he said *you are beautiful,* it was deeper
than high cheek bones, curved hips, soft
moans or compliments issued
as one part of a bargain. If an acerbic tone
caused him to stumble, or consider
walking away, he never did. Not really. How could he
leave a home he worked so hard to restore?
Questioning this and contemplating that,
he stripped me down—clothes, self-doubt,
labels I held too close that weren't mine.
At first, I fought the probing, the attention.
(I wasn't used to it). Didn't ask why
he thought I was worth it. Couldn't challenge
his conviction. (Didn't want to.) How could I
throw a brick through the walls we had restored
together, when I'd begun to believe.

When at last I understood
that being my own woman is a house
I must build from scratch, must choose,
every brick, must reject most donations for,
I started with what I knew—one morning,
when a full moon tinted the ocean
silver-white, we marvelled
at its splendour. I caught him gazing
at my face with the same awe. This isn't
about him, but the way he loved me with no
remorse was impressive. I wanted to love
myself like that. I gave up the craft
of busyness for its own sake, courted silence
until I wasn't afraid to be still, to stare
at my own face, my own body, beyond skin,
and be confronted with shame I'd accepted
without question—all the things they said
a real woman was that I wasn't.
The shame I owned for wanting
to opine without apology, though not for empty
attention, to love my own deep voice,
the roundness in my face that no diet would shed.
When the borrowed and donated things
were as tangible as a false wall, I pulled them down.
I now know where the floorboards creak,
which doors are not good for access, which jarring
paint I refuse to change, what it feels like
to be at peace with myself, all of myself.

Museum of Women

Praise for the mothers, their love
like an expensive scrub, scraping away
what is dead and what needs
to die, soothing the afterburn.

Praise for the sisters who show up
without needing to ask what is wrong,
arms full of plantains—portable joy,
who swathe your body before it can fall apart.

Praise for the women who write
books about women who challenge
us to live beyond survival; for the girls
whose stories incite renaissance.

Praise for all the women, who chorus
groans when the truth is too heavy for words.
Artists, quietly moulding, mending,
retouching me into a masterpiece, even when

I don't yet acknowledge I am still under construction.
If I ever said I made it this far alone, I lied.

Moments

Years later, when you think you have forgotten
he comes to you in a dream.

> Saturday morning. Mop at rest,
> you catch your face reflecting from the polished
> kitchen floor tiles. His face appears,
> hands at your waist. Then your bodies
> are falling, rolling, grabbing the air
> and each other, wrapped in bleach and pine,
> laughter and lavender, entwined
> and twisted in discovery.

Awake with memory, you recall how even then,
surrendering to the moment's ease, you knew
joy would always reside there—where you wrestled
like children for the fun of it, free and feeling
a nameless thing surging between you, stumbling
on a new level of comfort, like the first time
you both sat in a long silence and it didn't swallow.

The Routes are Many

And when the night calls me
not to bed, but casts its light over
the little-used ironing board—an invitation
to lay hands over perturbed thoughts,
choose what will continue to take
up space or burn, or be put away.

And when I succumb,
gripping the iron, the cloth, hope
bound in the motion of a hand passing
heat left to right over a crease, willing it
to disappear as proof that the dishevelled
can be smoothed again, what is it
if not prayer?

The Gift

Ask any kitchen she's commanded.
Ask me—I had to watch her. Only girl
between boys, traditions predating
my mother catapulted me to her kitchen,
voice rattling my ears if ever I risked absence.

&

I will remember the butter, ata rodo, plantain,
Maggi, tomatoes, the times she borrowed my hands,
the blender whirring, the oil sizzling, the way she split
herself in five no fuss as though her body knew
better than to stand in the way.

&

A tall pot masters its place on a high flame,
boils its water, threatens
to poach unshielded hands.

&

Last week, I conjured a meal for 70
in three hours—moving like Harmattan.
My mother showed her face.

Discovering My Name

An hour after he starts shampooing his metallic blue Skoda
Octavia, he crouches by each tyre, washing the wheel trims,
polishing what no one else will see, sparing no effort.
It's the same in the supermarket, when he lifts each fruit,
attentive to where it gives, what it holds back in scent
where to place it so it doesn't bruise. This is how
he carries my name—T, Tolu, Tolulola.

Light

(After painting 'Caring' by Jacqueline L. Patten-Van Sertima)

Painting a small room anything but white
invites a grim darkness—carob hued

walls advancing, their limbs jumping
off the last spot of light. Choking the air.

Sometimes you want this. You want
to be the body refereeing the fight,

arms starred out in a room
small enough to feel, when you have

lost capacity to feel yourself.
Sometimes in the belly of darkness

you cradle another life and watch
its joy light your face. This morning

I kept three fish alive. Shrouded in white,
bowing my body over their tank, I sprinkled

food and watched them shimmy a rainbow
through the water to have their fill.

This morning I smiled. This morning
I painted the room white.

Notes

1. *Obìrin bí ọkunrin/ Ajónirun / masu kunan bakin wake / kisan kai*—from the poem '**Before the Bomb Blast**'— Yoruba phrase meaning 'tomboy' / Yoruba phrase meaning 'that which consumes by burning' / Hausa phrases meaning 'suicide bomber' and 'suicide'.

2. Lines for the '**Cento**' were borrowed from the following poets in this order: Elizabeth Jennings (Rembrandt's Late Self Portraits), Rainer Maria Rilke (Archaic Torso of Apollo), lucille clifton (the thirty eight year), Derek Mahon (Ignorance), Norman MacCaig (February Not Everywhere), Doug Anderson (Night Ambush), Nikki Giovanni (Quilts) and Jack Mapanje (Skipping Without Ropes).

3. *Ça va? Pleus pas euh. N'est pas obligé le sexe mais tu peut me faire une pipe quand meme*—*from the poem* '**Locating Strongwoman**'—French phrase meaning 'Are you okay? Don't cry. We don't have to have sex but you could at least give me a blow job'

Acknowledgments

Thanks are due to the editors of the following publications in which different versions of these poems have appeared: *Filigree: Contemporary Black British Poetry* ('Faking Death To Avoid Sex Is Not Extreme'), *Pittsburgh Poetry Review* ('Light', 'We All Take Risks Stepping Into Thin Air', 'The Gift'), *The White Review* ('Locating Strongwoman), *Brittle Paper & Shado* ('Museum of Women').

Many of these poems were birthed and or found new life in poetry communities. I'm grateful to the Home Sessions family, Malika's Poetry Kitchen and to the 2016 Callaloo Creative Writing Fellowship cohort under the guidance of Vievee Francis.

Thank you to vangile gantsho for reading and giving honest critique in those early days when I questioned whether this manuscript had legs, Karen McCarthy Woolf for your input and Jemilea Wisdom-Baako, Shade Joseph, Naana Orleans-Amissah and Emmanuel Nwosu for reading and reading again, sometimes at crazy hours when I was struggling to make sense.

Special thanks to Vievee Francis for reminding me there is power and purpose in my poetic voice.

To Mum and Dad who don't always understand this poetry thing, but support it wholeheartedly; To my brothers and the sisters they gave me; To Mr and Mrs T, Ruth, Michelle S, Shirley, you all hold me up, I love you.

This book wouldn't have happened (not like this) without Jacob Sam-La Rose. Thank you for seeing me, respecting my work, for the suggestions, critique, honesty, the challenge of it all and for lessons that transcend editing this collection.

To all the women who dare daily to live out loud, thank you.

About the Author

Tolu Agbelusi is a Nigerian British poet, playwright, producer, educator and lawyer. Shortlisted for the 2018 White Review Poetry Prize, she is a 2016 Callaloo Creative Writing Fellow (Poetry). Her debut play, *Ilé La Wà* was produced & toured the UK between 2016 – 2019 to rave reviews. She is the founder of Home Sessions a poetry development and community-building programme for young Black writers. Tolu also facilitates a range of live literature, creative writing and poetry programmes with schools, festivals, universities, arts centres and other institutions.

Locating Strongwoman (Jacaranda Books) is her first collection. Visit www.ToluAgbelusi.com for more information.